LESSONS *from* LEVITICUS

A 30-day Devotional of Wisdom
from the Book of Leviticus
(Chapters 1-7)
-Volume One-

Jean Kabasomi

© Jean Kabasomi 2021. All rights reserved.
Jean Kabasomi has asserted her right under the Copyright, Design and Patents Act, 1988, to be identified as author of this work.

Unless otherwise indicated, all Scripture quotations are taken from New International Reader's Version (NIrV), copyright © 1995, 1996, 1998, 2014 by Biblica, Inc.® Used by permission. All rights reserved worldwide.

Other Scripture quotations are taken from:
New Living Translation (NLT), copyright © 1960, 1962, 1963, 1968, 1971, 1972, 1973, 1975, 1977, 1995 by The Lockman Foundation. Used by permission. www.Lockman.org.

New American Standard Bible® (NASB), copyright © 1960, 1971, 1977, 1995, 2020 by The Lockman Foundation. All rights reserved.

Cover design by 100 Covers
Interior design by Formatted Books

Contents

Acknowledgements.. i
A Few Notes by Way of Introduction iii

Day 1	Bring my Own Offering 1
Day 2	Bring your Best Offering....................................... 3
Day 3	Where Should I Give my Offering?...................... 7
Day 4	The Role of a Priest in our Offerings.................... 9
Day 5	Roles of the Priesthood 11
Day 6	Types of Offering... 13
Day 7	Insignificant Offerings..17
Day 8	My Offering is to be Eaten by the Priest 19
Day 9	My Tithe is a Tool of Remembrance 23
Day 10	The Ultimate Offering and Atonement 25
Day 11	Groupthink and Sin... 27
Day 12	The High Priest and Offering.............................. 31
Day 13	Honesty 35
Day 14	Integrity and my Neighbour 37
Day 15	Uncleanness 39

Day 16	Integrity and God	41
Day 17	Separation for God	43
Day 18	Obedience to God	45
Day 19	Holding Back	47
Day 20	Unfaithfulness to God	49
Day 21	Reconciliation and Worship	51
Day 22	Continuous Offerings	53
Day 23	Holiness and the Offering	55
Day 24	Full-time Ministry and the Offering	57
Day 25	Promotion, Anointing and the Offering	59
Day 26	Importance of the Sin Offering	61
Day 27	Friendship Offerings	63
Day 28	Timeliness and Offerings	65
Day 29	The Anointing of Others and my Response	67
Day 30	Direction from God	69

Also by Jean Kabasomi..71
About the Author..73

Acknowledgements

I would first like to thank God for the gift and opportunity to write.

I would also like to thank Bishop Dag Heward-Mills for introducing me to the New International Reader's Version of the Bible and for encouraging our church to use the book of Leviticus for our quiet times.

Finally, I would like to thank Dr David Reimer, my personal tutor during my master's course at the University of Edinburgh. Thank you, Dr Reimer, for teaching me that the Old Testament has its own valid independent voice. Thank you for teaching me to take a step back from the years of history between the Old and New Testaments and for asking me to think about how the text was meant to be understood and read before there was a New Testament.

A Few Notes by Way of Introduction

I would be lying if I said the Lord instructed me to write a devotional from the book of Leviticus. This wasn't my idea at all. During the COVID-19 lockdown period, our online church services and prayer meetings have been led by the founder of our church, Bishop Dag Heward-Mills. Towards the end of 2020, he suggested that we as a church read through Leviticus during our devotional (quiet) times. I decided to give it a go. Knowing that Leviticus is one of the more challenging texts in the Bible; I chose to use the most plain-speaking version of the Bible I could find and landed on the New International Reader's Version (NIrV).

To my surprise, I found that things seemed to be making sense. The Holy Spirit was indeed revealing practical insight that I could apply directly in my daily walk with the Lord. Despite receiving my own revelation and instruction by the Holy Spirit, I noticed that a few other members in my church were struggling to gain much, if anything, from the text. It was at this point that I felt led to share my notes with others through this series of devotionals.

To be clear, these devotionals are not intended to be biblical exegeses on the difficult, complex and often controversial topics found in the book of Leviticus such as homosexuality, sexual immorality, animal sacrifice, tattoos and piercings. Nor are they Bible commentaries which hope to answer questions or offer comments on which bits of the law apply today and which are to be rejected or ignored. Instead, this is a series of personal quiet times which seek to make the book of Leviticus more accessible and readable by the average Christian.

For the most part, I have tried to stick to the text of Leviticus. There is not much appeal to the New Testament, because this is supposed to be a devotional based on the book of Leviticus. That being said, there were moments during my quiet times where the Holy Spirit prompted me or reminded me of a parallel between the Leviticus passage for that day and a verse in the New Testament. Where that is the case, I have included the relevant New Testament passage in the reading for the day.

Also, for Christians there are passages within Leviticus which are superseded by the coming of Jesus as the Messiah – specifically, passages relating to atonement, guilt and sin offerings, and the role of the high priest. In these instances, I have tried to convey that these passages are precursors for what Christ did for us on the cross. Christ is now our eternal High Priest who gave Himself once to atone for all our guilt and sin. When we read these passages, we are to be reminded of this sacrifice rather than of our sin and note that we do not need to and cannot pay for our sin. This has already been done for us at Calvary.

Finally, a few words on the structure. Every day there is a verse to be read for reflection and prayer. This is then followed by my thoughts and interpretation. Each reflection ends with one or two questions for you to consider about how the passage may or may not impact your daily walk with the Lord. All use of bold italics through the Bible citations is my emphasis.

I pray that this devotional will be a blessing and that the Lord Himself will open your eyes so that you may see wondrous things in His Word.

In Him we move,
Jean

DAY 1

Bring my Own Offering

Leviticus 1:1–4 - The Lord called out to Moses. He spoke to him from the tent of meeting. He said, "Speak to the Israelites. Tell them, 'Suppose anyone among you brings an offering to the Lord. They must ***bring an animal from their*** herd or flock. If someone brings a burnt offering from the herd, they must offer a male animal. It must not have any flaws. They must bring it to the entrance to the tent of meeting. Then the Lord will accept it. ***They must place their hand on the head of the burnt offering.*** Then the Lord will accept it in place of them. It will pay for their sin.'"

In the opening verses of the book of Leviticus, the Lord instructs Moses on the rules of offering. Offerings are optional; they are not a requirement like the tithe. But in the event that someone brings an offering, it must be from *their own* herd or flock. Any offering that we present to the Lord must be from what we own and not from someone else. There must be a direct connection between me and what I present to the Lord.

The Lord's instructions to Moses included a requirement that the bringer of the offering place his hand on the head of the animal. This connection facilitated the acceptance of the offering by God.

Many well-meaning parents often ignore this principle. I am sure, like me, you have seen parents reach into their purses, wallets or pockets and hand their children an offering for the children's service. However, although well meaning, this approach is not biblical. Instead, children are to be encouraged to prepare their own offering from any weekly allowance/pocket money they receive and present their offering from this.

Another common, well-meaning mistake is the giving of offerings on behalf of a spouse or partner. As we have already seen, each person is supposed to bring *their own* offering before the Lord. Just as we all have an individual personal relationship with the Lord, we are each supposed to have an individual personal *offering* relationship with the Lord.

Questions: Is my offering my own? Is there a direct connection between my offering and me? Am I teaching my children to give out of their own – what belongs to them?

DAY 2

Bring your Best Offering

Leviticus 1:3 - If someone brings a burnt offering from the herd, they must offer a male animal. ***It must not have any flaws.*** They must bring it to the entrance to the tent of meeting. Then the LORD will accept it.

Leviticus 1:10 - If someone offers a burnt offering from the flock, it must be a male animal. It can be a sheep or a goat. ***It must not have any flaws.***

Leviticus 2:1 - Suppose anyone brings a grain offering to the LORD. ***Then their offering must be made out of the finest flour.*** They must pour olive oil on it. They must also put incense on it.

Yesterday, we looked at bringing our own offering to the Lord, but that is not the end of the instruction to Moses. Not only should it be a personal offering, but our offerings must be our very best. The offerings presented to the Lord were supposed to be without flaws. We see the importance of this criterion by the fact that it is mentioned twice in the same chapter. Most of us give offerings from our own salaries or income, but can we honestly say that every time we give an offering it is our very best? Often, we give whatever happens to be in reach – whatever we happen to find on our person, in our bags, wallets or purses. If we are giving online during an e-service, we may find it inconvenient to access our online banking, and say to ourselves that we will give later, but then forget. This is not what it means to give our best to the Lord; to give an offering without flaws.

One way to give our best to the Lord might be to prepare how much we will give (of course this may change during the service if one is led to give more). To fulfil the instruction given by the Lord, to bring an offering without flaws, the giver would have had to inspect their animal *before* presenting to the Lord. This would have been the only way to know that the animal did not have any blemishes and that it indeed was the very best animal to give to the Lord. Perhaps, if we prepare our offerings, thoughtfully and in prayer we may find that we are led to give an offering that costs us and represents our best.

Recently, I was budgeting and looking at my outgoings. I remembered that as a student, I had always wanted to give a set weekly offering but couldn't afford to. As I looked at my spreadsheet, I asked myself why I wasn't giving that amount and, if not now, when exactly would I give that offering? How much would I need to earn before I felt comfortable in giving that amount? I then realised I would always have a reason not to give that amount, and decided to give that amount.

Another way to determine whether we are giving our best, is to consider whether or not *we* would be happy to receive the offering we have given. Of course, we all have various giving capacities, so the amount is not what we are considering here. We also know that God is concerned with the heart of the giver more than the amount given. But for those of us who are giving less than we ought to, reflecting on the amount may cause us to give something that is more representative of our best.

Questions: Do I give my very best offerings to the Lord? When was the last time I prepared or reviewed my giving? Are my offerings an afterthought? How often do I forget to follow through during an online service and give an offering?

DAY 3

Where Should I Give my Offering?

Leviticus 1:3 - If someone brings a burnt offering from the herd, they must offer a male animal. It must not have any flaws. ***They must bring it to the entrance to the tent of meeting.*** Then the LORD will accept it.

We live in a generation which has more freedom and liberty than ever before. This freedom stems across all facets of our lives, including where and how we spend our money. However, this freedom, plus our society's lack of trust in the Church and Christianity generally, has led many of us into a misplaced view that our offerings can be given to any good cause and not necessarily to the Church.

This is a mistake; in today's passage we see that the offering was to be brought to the entrance of the tent of meeting. Offerings are to be given in the place where we meet God. For us, that means the Church – your local church. This does not mean that we can't or should not give to charitable causes or help out people in our community who require financial assistance, but it does mean that we should see that type of giving as separate and different from our offerings, which we are to give to the Lord in His house.

Question: Do I give an offering in my local church – my tent of meeting?

DAY 4

The Role of a Priest in our Offerings

Leviticus 1:3–9 - If someone brings a burnt offering from the herd, they must offer a male animal. It must not have any flaws. They must bring it to the entrance to the tent of meeting. Then the LORD will accept it. They must place their hand on the head of the burnt offering. Then the LORD will accept it in place of them. It will pay for their sin. The young bull must be killed there in the sight of the LORD. ***Then the priests in Aaron's family line*** must bring its blood to the altar. They must splash it against the sides of the altar. The altar stands at the entrance to the tent of meeting. The skin must be removed from the animal brought for the burnt offering. Then the animal must be cut into pieces. ***The priests in Aaron's family line*** must build a fire on the altar. They must place wood on the fire. Then they must place the pieces of the animal on the burning wood on the altar. The pieces include the head and the fat. The inside parts of the animal must be washed with water. The legs must also be washed. ***The priest must burn all of it on the altar.*** It is a burnt offering. It is a food offering. Its smell pleases the LORD.

Perhaps one of the most controversial topics in modern Christianity is the relationship between pastors/priests and money. But here in this passage, we see that there is a clear role for priests in the handling of the offerings given to God. As believers, our role is to bring the offering to our local church; it is then the responsibility of the designated members of the church leadership to handle our offerings. This is not to excuse bad stewardship of offerings, but is to remind us that we should not be influenced by what the world says about the workings of the Church of God.

I go to a church which is transparent about how and where our offerings are spent. For some churches, high levels of transparency are not possible due to political or legal reasons within the country where the church operates. That being said, whether you are like me and have full transparency or not, we all need to accept and believe that there is a role for priests to influence how offerings are spent. If we are able to accept this and believe that God is totally in control, where there is bad stewardship concerning finances, we can be sure that we have done our part and God will deal with the rest accordingly.

Questions: Have I accepted the stewardship and role of the priesthood concerning my offerings? Does my lack of acceptance prevent me from giving my best? Do I need to renew my mind concerning giving?

DAY 5

Roles of the Priesthood

Leviticus 1:7 - **The priests in Aaron's family line** must build a fire on the altar. They must place wood on the fire.

Leviticus 4:13–21 - Or suppose the whole community of Israel sins without meaning to. They do something the Lord commands us not to do. Suppose they realize their guilt. And suppose their sin becomes known. Then they must bring a young bull as a sin offering. They must offer it in front of the tent of meeting. The elders of the community must place their hands on the bull's head in the sight of the Lord. The bull must be killed in the sight of the Lord. Then the ***anointed priest*** must take some of the bull's blood into the tent of meeting. He must dip his finger into the blood. He must sprinkle it seven times in the sight of the Lord. He must do it in front of the curtain. He must put some of the blood on the horns that stick out from the upper four corners of the altar. The altar stands in front of the LORD in the tent of meeting. The priest must pour out the rest of the blood at the bottom of the altar for burnt offerings. That altar stands at the entrance to the tent. He must remove all the fat from the bull. He must burn it on the altar. He must do the same thing with that bull as he did with the bull for the sin offering. When he does, he will pay for the sin of the community. And they will be forgiven. Then he must take the bull outside the camp. He must burn it just as he burned the first bull. It is the sin offering for the whole community.

We are all equal, but not the same. Every one of us has a different and unique role to play in the house of God. In these passages we see that this applies to the priesthood too. Not all priests were involved in the preparation of the offerings and altar. Among the Levites, it was specifically the sons of Aaron who were assigned this duty. Similarly, in Leviticus 4, we see that the anointed priest (high priest in other translations) was responsible for dealing with the preparation of the sin offering.

Not everyone has the same role or function in the Church. There are some roles reserved for specific people. Rank has always been something to be observed by the people of God. The high priest sat in a unique seat. This role was separate and different from the role of the other priests. As the people of God, we must respect the order and functions that God has laid out for us as His Church.

Questions: Am I content with the role God has given me in my local church? Do I respect the roles and functions of my church leadership? Do I accept that while we are all equal before God, we are not all the same?

DAY 6

Types of Offering

Leviticus 1:3–9 - If someone brings a burnt offering from the herd, they must offer a male animal. It must not have any flaws. They must bring it to the entrance to the tent of meeting. Then the Lord will accept it. They must place their hand on the head of the burnt offering. Then the Lord will accept it in place of them. It will pay for their sin. The young bull must be killed there in the sight of the Lord. Then the priests in Aaron's family line must bring its blood to the altar. They must splash it against the sides of the altar. The altar stands at the entrance to the tent of meeting. The skin must be removed from the animal brought for the burnt offering. Then the animal must be cut into pieces. The priests in Aaron's family line must build a fire on the altar. They must place wood on the fire. Then they must place the pieces of the animal on the burning wood on the altar. The pieces include the head and the fat. The inside parts of the animal must be washed with water. The legs must also be washed. The priest must burn all of it on the altar. It is a ***burnt offering***. It is a ***food offering***. Its smell pleases the LORD.

Leviticus 2:4–10 - If you bring a ***grain offering*** baked in an oven, make it out of the finest flour. It can be ***thick loaves of bread made without yeast***. Mix them with olive oil. Or it can be ***thin loaves of bread that are made without yeast***. Spread olive oil on them. If your ***grain offering is cooked on a metal plate***, make your offering out of the finest flour. Mix it with oil. Make it without yeast. Break it into pieces. Pour oil on it. It is a grain offering. If ***your grain offering is cooked in a pan***, make your offering ***out of the finest flour and some olive oil. Bring to the LORD your grain offering made out of all these things.*** Give it to the priest. He must take it to the altar. All good things come from the LORD. The priest must take out the part of the grain offering that reminds you of this. He must burn it on the altar. It is a food offering. Its smell pleases the LORD. The rest of the grain offering belongs to Aaron and the priests in his family line. It is a very holy part of the food offerings presented to the LORD.

So far, we have only considered financial offerings, but actually the Lord accepts whatever we have to offer him. All that is required of offerings is that they cost us, are our very best and are offered in His house. Here, we see that the grain offering was accepted in not just different forms, but also cooked in more than one way.

There are many ways that we can give an offering to God. For some of us it might be our education or skills. Perhaps we can offer to do the church accounting at a discounted rate or for no charge? Maybe we can help with social media marketing, website design or with the church choir? Perhaps we can use our baking and cooking skills at a church event? Or we can open up our home, garage or basement for a church meeting or rehearsal? All of these are examples of non-financial offerings that we can offer to the Lord.

Questions: Have I ever considered giving a non-financial offering to the Lord? What skills do I have that I can offer to the Lord? What do I have that can be presented to the Lord as a gift?

DAY 7

Insignificant Offerings

Leviticus 1:12–13 - They must cut the animal into pieces. The priest must place the pieces on the burning wood on the altar. The pieces include the head and the fat. They must wash the inside parts with water. The legs must also be washed. The priest must bring all the parts to the altar. He must burn them there. It is a burnt offering. It is a food offering. Its ***smell pleases the Lord***.

In today's passage, we see that the priest when preparing the animal for the burnt offering was to use all of it. There was no insignificant part of the animal. All was to be burnt and offered to the Lord. Even the smell of the offering was pleasing to God. What does this mean for us today? It means that there is no insignificant offering. There is no offering that is too small to give to God. No offering is non-valuable. God is not concerned with the amount but rather that it is the very best that you and I can give. Jesus made this point to the disciples when He saw the poor widow give her offering.

Luke 21:1–4 - While Jesus was in the Temple, he watched the rich people dropping their gifts in the collection box. ***Then a poor widow came by and dropped in two small coins.*** "I tell you the truth," Jesus said, "***this poor widow has given more than all the rest of them***. For they have given a tiny part of their surplus, but she, ***poor as she is, has given everything she has.***" (NLT)

Questions: Do I think about the value of my offering rather than whether it is my best? Do I think my offering is insignificant because I am comparing myself with others? Am I willing to give despite what I have rather than because of what I have?

DAY 8

My Offering is to be Eaten by the Priest

Leviticus 2:1–3 - Suppose anyone brings a grain offering to the LORD. Then their offering must be made out of the finest flour. They must pour olive oil on it. They must also put incense on it. They must take it to the priests in Aaron's family line. A priest must take a handful of the flour and oil. He must mix them with all the incense. Then he must burn that part on the altar. It will be a reminder that all good things come from the LORD. It is a food offering. Its smell pleases the LORD. ***The rest of the grain offering belongs to Aaron and to the priests in his family line.*** It is a ***very holy*** part of the food offerings presented to the LORD.

A few days ago, we saw that contrary to the views of society today, there is a role for the priesthood in the handling of offerings. In today's passage we see that the Lord intended for priests to receive part of the offering for themselves and their families. As believers, we must renew our minds and accept that part of our offerings to the Lord belongs to the priesthood.

The majority of the grain offering belongs to the priests. Only a handful of this offering is offered to the Lord by the priest. We are also told that the part that belongs to Aaron and the priests in his family is a very holy part of the food offerings presented to the Lord. This instruction is repeated in both Leviticus 6 and 7.

> Leviticus 6:14–18 - Here are some more rules for grain offerings. The priests in Aaron's family line must bring the grain offering to the LORD in front of the altar. The priest must take a handful of the finest flour and olive oil. He must add to it all the incense on the grain offering. He must burn that part on the altar. It will remind him that all good things come from the LORD. Its smell pleases the LORD. ***Aaron and the priests in his family line will eat the rest of it.*** But they must eat it without yeast in the holy area. They must eat it in the courtyard of the tent of meeting. It must not be baked with yeast added to it. ***The LORD has given it to the priests as their share of the food offerings presented to him.*** It is ***very holy***, just like the sin offering and the guilt offering. Any priests in Aaron's family line can eat it. ***It is their share of the food offerings presented to the LORD. It is their share for all time to come. Anyone who touches these offerings will become holy.***
>
> Leviticus 7:28–35 - The LORD spoke to Moses. He said, "Speak to the Israelites. Tell them, 'Suppose someone brings a friendship offering to the LORD. Then they must bring part of it as their special gift to the LORD.

Lessons from Leviticus

They must bring it with their own hands. It is a food offering presented to the LORD. They must bring the fat together with the breast. They must lift the breast up and wave it in front of the LORD as a wave offering. The priest will burn the fat on the altar. ***But the breast belongs to Aaron and the priests in his family line.*** Give the ***right thigh from your friendship offerings to the priest as a gift***. The priest who offers the blood and fat from the friendship offering must be given the right thigh. ***It is his share. I, the LORD, have taken the breast that is waved and the thigh that is given. I have taken them from the friendship offerings of the Israelites. And I have given them to Aaron the priest and the priests in his family line. The offerings will be their share from the Israelites for all time to come.*** " That is the part of the food offerings presented to the LORD. It is given to Aaron and the priests in his family line. ***It was given to Aaron and his sons on the day they were set apart to serve the LORD as priests.***

What does this all mean for us today? We don't give grain or animal offerings, so we must accept that our monetary offerings in part belong to the church leadership. Not only does some of our offering belong to our pastors and priests, but God views this part of our offering as *very holy*, contrary to what the world thinks. We must accept that God's ways are not the same as the ways of the world. The Lord is concerned with the well-being of his servants and, as such, has decided that a section of our offerings belongs to them. Please understand this: I am not arguing for or supporting the misuse of church finances or offerings. Instead, I am asking us to reflect on our understanding of how church leadership is remunerated.

Jean Kabasomi

Many of us have held the view that priests should not be paid, but here we see that the Lord purposefully set aside a portion of the offering for his servants.

Questions: Do I have the right attitude towards my offering and church leadership? Am I influenced by the world or God's Word on this topic? Do I need to renew my mind in this area?

DAY 9

My Tithe is a Tool of Remembrance

Leviticus 2:14–16 - Suppose you bring to the Lord a ***grain offering*** of the ***first*** share of your food. Then offer crushed heads of your ***first*** grain that have been cooked in fire. Put olive oil and incense on the grain. It is a grain offering. The priest must burn part of the crushed grain and the oil. ***It will remind you that all good things come from the Lord.*** The priest must burn it together with all the incense. It is a food offering presented to the Lord.

Throughout the Hebrew Bible (Old Testament), we are reminded to bring our first fruits to the Lord. This is typically referred to and understood as the same as tithe; namely 10 per cent of one's increase. Here we are told that when we present our tithes to the Lord, they are to act as a reminder that all good things come from the Lord. Rather than a weekly or monthly routine, the giving of our tithe should invoke the spirit of remembrance. We are to remember (among his many other benefits), that it is God who gives us the power to gain wealth.

Questions: Is my tithe-paying a box-ticking exercise? Does my tithe-giving provoke the spirit of remembrance? Am I grateful for all the good things that come from the Lord? Do I think about how the Lord has blessed me?

DAY 10

The Ultimate Offering and Atonement

Leviticus 4:1–3 - The Lord spoke to Moses. He said, "Speak to the Israelites. Tell them, 'Suppose someone sins without meaning to. And that person does something the Lord commands us not to do. Suppose it is the anointed priest who sins. And suppose he brings guilt on the people. Then he must bring a young bull to the Lord. It must not have any flaws. ***He must bring it as a sin offering for the sin he has committed.**'"

Leviticus 4:22–24 - Or suppose a leader sins without meaning to. He disobeys any of the commands of the Lord his God. ***And suppose he realizes his guilt and his sin becomes known. Then he must bring an offering.*** It must be a male goat. It must not have any flaws. He must place his hand on the goat's head. He must kill it. He must do it at the place where the animals for burnt offerings are killed in the sight of the Lord. His offering is a sin offering.

Jean Kabasomi

Unlike the Israelites who lived in a time before Christ, we are no longer required to give a sin offering every time we sin intentionally or mistakenly. Instead, we know and believe that Jesus Christ paid the ultimate price and became the ultimate offering for our sin, taking away our debt. However, just like the Israelites, we still sin daily. The recurring theme in the New Testament on sin is not sacrifice, but to regularly pray for forgiveness. Jesus taught us to pray to the Father for forgiveness. John wrote that God is faithful and just in that He forgives us of our sins if we confess them and the author of Hebrews encouraged us to approach the throne of grace for mercy in our time of need.

Today, we are not required to sacrifice but to ask for forgiveness and to live a life of repentance.

Questions: Do I truly believe that Jesus' sacrifice is enough to make up for all my mistakes and past sins? When was the last time I prayed for forgiveness? Have I asked God to forgive me for the sins that I have committed accidentally and intentionally? Have I accepted that although I will make mistakes, there is grace and mercy to help me overcome my mistakes if I ask for God's help?

DAY 11

Groupthink and Sin

Leviticus 4:13–14 - Or suppose ***the whole community of Israel sins*** without meaning to. They do something the Lord commands us not to do. Suppose they realize their guilt. And suppose their sin becomes known. Then they must bring a young bull as a sin offering. They must offer it in front of the tent of meeting.

In modern Christianity, we often speak of our individual sin and need to seek God for both forgiveness and grace. This is not to condemn us, but to prompt us to live lives that are pleasing to God and reflect his impact on our lives. However, we rarely if ever speak of our community or group sins. Whether we like it or not, we all have a way of thinking or doing things based on the world around us. Our outlook is different based on our gender, upbringing, denomination, age, generation, location, vocation and family background. Often, we gravitate towards people who are most like us, which can inadvertently lead us to people who think just like us and into a phenomenon known as groupthink.

The Oxford online dictionary defines groupthink as:

> The practice of thinking or making decisions as a group, resulting typically in unchallenged, poor-quality decision-making.*

Since the global financial crisis, many commentators have suggested that the behaviour and practices of those in the financial industry at the time can be attributed to groupthink. What seemed normal and proper to those who worked in the sector was deemed totally unacceptable to those who operated outside it. The financial sector was blind to its flaws because everyone thought, looked, dressed, behaved the same. It would be naïve for us not to think that, just as those in the financial sector in 2008 were blind to their collective 'sin', so we too are oblivious to our sins that are caused or influenced by the groups we belong to.

For every group we belong to, we must ask ourselves: does my association with this group cause me to think in a way that is contrary to the word of God? It is this constant review that prevents us from unknowingly falling into group sin.

Questions: Does my thinking need to be renewed because of the natural groups I belong to? Could I be committing a groupthink 'sin'? What are the common distractions and delusions associated with people like me? Groupings to consider:

a) Gender

---

* 'groupthink' – Lexico.com (12 April 2021). www.lexico.com/definition/groupthink

b) Denomination
c) Age
d) Generation
e) Marital status
f) Occupation
g) Location
h) Race
i) Family background

DAY 12

The High Priest and Offering

Leviticus 4:2–3 - Speak to the Israelites. Tell them, 'Suppose someone sins without meaning to. And that person does something the LORD commands us not to do. ***Suppose it is the anointed priest who sins. And suppose he brings guilt on the people. Then he must bring a young bull to the LORD.*** It must not have any flaws. He must bring it as a sin offering for the sin he has committed.'

Leviticus 4:16–20 - Then the anointed priest must take some of the bull's blood into the tent of meeting. He must dip his finger into the blood. He must sprinkle it seven times in the sight of the LORD. He must do it in front of the curtain. He must put some of the blood on the horns that stick out from the upper four corners of the altar. The altar stands in front of the LORD in the tent of meeting. The priest must pour out the rest of the blood at the bottom of the altar for burnt offerings.

That altar stands at the entrance to the tent. He must remove all the fat from the bull. He must burn it on the altar. He must do the same thing with that bull as he did with the bull for the sin offering. ***When he does, he will pay for the sin of the community.*** And they will be forgiven.

Hebrews 7:19–28 - For the law never made anything perfect. But now we have confidence in a better hope, through which we draw near to God. This new system was established with a solemn oath. Aaron's descendants became priests without such an oath, but there was an oath regarding Jesus. For God said to him,

"The Lord has taken an oath and will not break his vow:

'You are a priest forever.'"

Because of this oath, ***Jesus is the one who guarantees this better covenant with God***. There were many priests under the old system, for death prevented them from remaining in office. But because Jesus lives forever, his priesthood lasts forever. Therefore, ***he is able, once and forever, to save those who come to God through him***. He lives forever to intercede with God on their behalf. He is the kind of high priest we need because he is holy and blameless, unstained by sin. He has been set apart from sinners and has been given the highest place of honor in heaven. ***Unlike those other high priests, he does not need to offer sacrifices every day.*** They did this for their own sins first and then for the sins of the people. ***But Jesus did this once for all when he offered himself as the sacrifice for the people's sins.*** The law appointed high priests who were limited by human weakness. But after the law was given, God appointed his Son with an oath, and ***his Son has been made the perfect High Priest forever.*** (NLT)

In today's Leviticus passages we see that there was a role for the anointed (high) priest in the offerings for sin for both himself and the people of Israel. As the passage in Hebrews explains, we are no longer to approach any person to assist us in an offering for our sin. Instead, Jesus as our High Priest acted once on our behalf. His one act of sacrifice lasts for all time. We can now approach the Father boldly, not because of anything we have done, but because of his everlasting sacrifice. All we have to do is accept this sacrifice and approach the Father boldly.

Questions: Am I constantly trying to do things to be accepted by God as well as people? Have I truly accepted that Jesus' sacrifice is complete and everlasting?

DAY 13

Honesty

Leviticus 5:1 - Suppose someone has been called as a witness to something they have seen or learned about. ***Then if they do not tell what they know, they have sinned.*** And they will be held responsible for it.

Honesty is broadly seen as a good virtue, not just in the Church, but in the world too. But many of us struggle to turn an admirable quality into an actuality. It's easy to tell the truth when it doesn't cost you anything or when it's in your favour. But when we are afraid or trying to save face many of us opt for what society calls a 'white lie'. Sometimes we even tell a partial truth to prevent others from being hurt or offended. However, this is not biblical. God expects us to tell the truth when called, whether it's in our interest or not, whether unintentionally hurts someone or not. If we do not tell what we know, then we have sinned. That being said, our truth must always be mixed with grace. Truth should not pull down or condemn. Truth comes to bring justice and correction, not guilt and shame.

Questions: Do I tell the truth when I am asked? Am I willing to being truthful, even when it costs me or someone I love? Is my truth mixed with grace?

DAY 14

Integrity and my Neighbour

Leviticus 5:4–5 - ***Or suppose someone makes a promise to do something without thinking it through.*** It does not matter what they promised. It does not matter whether they made the promise without thinking about it carefully. And suppose they are not aware that they did not think it through. When they find out about it, they will be guilty. ***When someone is guilty in any of those ways, they must admit they have sinned.***

Perhaps one of the easiest traps to fall into is to overcommit oneself. Many of us are well meaning but find ourselves disappointing those we have reached out to. Here we see that even if we are well meaning and have miscalculated, we are still wrong. When we find ourselves in this position, we are to turn back, admit we had spoken too quickly and reassess our commitments. In the words of our Saviour, our yes is supposed to mean yes and our no is supposed to mean no.

Jean Kabasomi

Questions: Do I regularly overextend myself? Do I have many outstanding commitments? Do I need to develop the art of saying no gracefully to avoid letting people down in the future?

DAY 15

Uncleanness

Leviticus 5:2–3 - ***Or suppose someone touches something not "clean."*** It could be the dead bodies of wild animals or of livestock. Or it could be the dead bodies of creatures that move along the ground. ***Even though those people are not aware that they touched them, they have become "unclean." And they are guilty.*** Or suppose they touch something "unclean" that comes from a human being. It could be anything that would make them "unclean." Suppose they are not aware that they touched it. When they find out about it, they will be guilty.

For many of us, when we wake up in the morning, we intend to live lives solely devoted to the Lord. We aim not to commit the same mistakes we made the day before. We plan to overcome envy, jealousy, anger, worldliness, lust, greed and sexual immorality, but fall at our first encounter either by way of our phone or in our personal exchanges with other people (whether Christians or non-Christians). Often, this is because of the environment we find ourselves in, rather than because of us on our own. The truth is, if we are constantly engaging with 'unclean' environments, the only outcome will be that we become unclean ourselves.

What does it mean for something to be unclean? There are some obvious examples – perhaps we have friends who do not believe in God and mock our relationship with God, causing us to do things we know to be wrong or to deny our faith. This is clearly an environment to move away from. Or we are watching films or TV shows which invoke feelings of lust or sexual immorality. Again, this is an environment that needs to be avoided. Maybe our scrolling through Instagram posts causes us to develop feelings of jealousy, envy, anxiety, ungratefulness, comparison, insignificance or unworthiness. This, too, is an environment that you may need to move away from. These are just a few examples; I am sure you can think of many others where you and I are mixing with what is unclean. Now that we have identified these areas, we must work to separate ourselves from the unclean, limiting its exposure in our daily routines.

Questions: What am I doing that is causing me to mix with what is unclean? How can I adapt my daily routines to minimise my exposure to what is unclean? Have I asked for God to help me overcome the areas of my life where I am mixing with the unclean?

DAY 16

Integrity and God

Leviticus 5:4–6 - Or suppose someone makes a promise to do something without thinking it through. It does not matter what they promised. It does not matter whether they made the promise without thinking about it carefully. And suppose they are not aware that they did not think it through. When they find out about it, they will be guilty. When someone is guilty in any of those ways, they must admit they have sinned. ***They must bring a sin offering to pay for the sin they have committed.*** They must bring to the LORD a female lamb or goat from the flock. The priest will sacrifice the animal. That will pay for the person's sin.

When we let people down, we usually apologise to the people we have let down but, in this passage, we are told that the people of God were supposed to make an offering to God after overcommitting themselves. This reveals to us that our integrity and word matter to God. Whenever we break our word, we become a little less believable to the people around us. As Christians, we are Christ's ambassadors, meaning that we are his representatives here on earth. Our truce-breaking does not only reflect badly on our own character, but also on the character of God. Perhaps this is why James wrote that our yes should mean yes and our no should mean no.

> James 5:12 - But most of all, my brothers and sisters, never take an oath, by heaven or earth or anything else. Just say a ***simple yes or no***, so that you will not sin and be condemned. (NLT)

Questions: How often do I break my word? Do I regularly overextend myself? Am I aware that by breaking my word I am reflecting both my own and God's character?

DAY 17

Separation for God

Leviticus 5:14–15 - The LORD spoke to Moses. He said, "Suppose someone is unfaithful to me and sins. And they do it without meaning to. *Here is how they sin against me or my priests. They refuse to give the priests one of the holy things set apart for them.* Then they must bring me a ram from the flock. It must not have any flaws. It must be worth the required amount of silver. The silver must be weighed out in keeping with the standard weights that are used in the sacred tent. The ram is a guilt offering. It will pay for their sin.

Most of us are aware of the separation process that we go through at the beginning of our walk with the Lord. Many of us find ourselves moving away from friends, music, environments and TV shows which are no longer appealing. But, in this passage, we see that there are items that we are called to set aside for use by God and his servants. Perhaps God has asked you to set aside your car for transportation of members on

Sunday mornings? Or maybe He has asked you to set aside your house for a midweek cell meeting? Maybe He has asked you to set aside your Friday evenings and phone allowance to call irregular church members in your local church?

Questions: What has God asked me to separate for His use? Have I separated what I need to separate for my church to use?

DAY 18

Obedience to God

Leviticus 8:9 - Then he placed the turban on Aaron's head. On the front of the turban, he put the gold plate. It was a sacred crown. ***Moses did everything just as the LORD had commanded him.***

I am in the middle of writing a book on Moses and his relationship with God, and I think the most striking feature of their relationship is Moses' obedience to whatever God instructed him to do. Throughout the books of Moses, we see God giving an instruction and Moses obeying that instruction. Whether it be approaching Pharaoh, parting the Red Sea, instructing the elders or the people of Israel, implementing the rules for the priesthood or creating the tabernacle – Moses was obedient to God.

Perhaps it was this characteristic that caused the Lord to speak to Moses as though he was His friend. From Moses, we learn that obedience to God is often difficult, challenging and contrary to what we want to do. But we also learn from

Jean Kabasomi

Moses that in obeying God, He can use us well beyond our wildest dreams.

Questions: What has the Lord asked me to do? Am I doing all that the Lord has asked me to do? Am I seeking God to find out what He wants me to do?

DAY 19

Holding Back

Leviticus 5:15–16 - *Suppose someone is unfaithful to me and sins. And they do it without meaning to. Here is how they sin against me or my priests. They refuse to give the priests one of the holy things set apart for them.* Then they must bring me a ram from the flock. It must not have any flaws. It must be worth the required amount of silver. The silver must be weighed out in keeping with the standard weights that are used in the sacred tent. The ram is a guilt offering. It will pay for their sin. They must also pay for the holy thing they refused to give. They must add a fifth of its value to it. They must give all of it to the priest. The priest will pay for their sin with the ram. It is a guilt offering. And they will be forgiven.

One of the things I have struggled with is holding back. We usually hold back when we are afraid of being hurt by the people around us. Unfortunately, many of us take this same attitude to God. We do not give ourselves completely, just in case it doesn't work out. We don't commit ourselves fully in either time or energy just in case it ends up being for nothing. Either the end result is poor or our time, energy or money is not valued by the people around us. We are afraid of hearing 'give more', 'this isn't good enough' or 'someone else would have done it better', so we hold back.

When we hold back, we usually have our eyes fixed on the wrong thing. Our eyes are usually fixed on the people around us rather than on the One who has called us. Just as in the parable of the talents, in the passage above we see that God is displeased by our holding back. Here, the people of God are required to pay back an extra 20 per cent of what they held back. In the parable of the talents, the unprofitable servant is cast into outer darkness. One of the things that has helped me in this area is to picture the Day of Judgement. Will I be able to say to the Lord with confidence, 'I did not do what you told me to do because I thought Sally would do it better'? Probably not.

Questions: Am I holding back in any area of my life? Do I hold back because of other people? Have I withdrawn in my local church? Do I think my actions/thoughts would stand up before the Lord?

DAY 20

Unfaithfulness to God

Leviticus 6:1–3 - The LORD spoke to Moses. He said, "Suppose someone sins by not being faithful to me. They do it by tricking their neighbors. They trick them in connection with something their neighbors have placed in their care. They steal from their neighbors. Or they cheat them. Or they find something their neighbors have lost and then tell a lie about it. Or they go to court. They promise to tell the truth. But instead, they tell a lie when they are a witness about it. Or they lie when they are witnesses about any other sin like those sins."

Like so many others in the Bible, this passage throws up a curveball. Before I read this passage, I did not think that unfaithfulness to God had anything to do with other people. I assumed it was connected to my relationship with Him only. When I read the first line of this verse, I was expecting the subsequent verses to be about idols and sacrifice. I suspect you thought the same too. But here as ever, I see how different I am to God. God's heart has always been and continues to be focused on His people. So, when His people (people generally) are treated unfairly, the Lord sees this as a personal attack. Here we see that stealing, lying, deceit and bearing false witness are not just sins against our neighbour, but are actually acts of unfaithfulness to God.

Questions: Have I been unfaithful to God by lying, stealing or bearing false witness against my neighbour? Do I treat people with respect?

DAY 21

Reconciliation and Worship

Leviticus 6:1–6 - The LORD spoke to Moses. He said, "Suppose someone sins by not being faithful to me. They do it by tricking their neighbors. They trick them in connection with something their neighbors have placed in their care. They steal from their neighbors. Or they cheat them. Or they find something their neighbors have lost and then tell a lie about it. Or they go to court. They promise to tell the truth. But instead they tell a lie when they are a witness about it. Or they lie when they are witnesses about any other sin like those sins. When they sin in any of these ways and realize their guilt, they must return what they stole. ***They must give back what they took by cheating their neighbors. They must return what their neighbors placed in their care.*** They must return the lost property they found. They must return anything they told a lie about when they were witnesses in court. They must pay back everything in full. They must add a fifth of its value to it. ***They must give all of it***

to the owner on the day they bring their guilt offering. He must bring their guilt offering to the priest to pay for their sin. It is an offering to me. They must bring a ram from the flock. It must not have any flaws. It must be worth the required amount of money."

As you may have noticed, much of what we find in the book of Leviticus can be found in one form or another in the New Testament, and more specifically in the words of Jesus. In today's passage we see that when the people of Israel had done wrong against their neighbour, they were to reconcile first with their neighbour before offering a sin offering to the Lord.

This is exactly what Christ taught us to do when we have a disagreement with our neighbour.

Matthew 5:23–24 - ***So if you are presenting a sacrifice at the altar in the Temple and you suddenly remember that someone has something against you, leave your sacrifice there at the altar. Go and be reconciled to that person. Then come and offer your sacrifice to God.*** (NLT)

Jesus' command to sort out any issue we may have with a neighbour before coming to God is not new. In Leviticus, the Israelites are expected to repent of their sins with God and with their fellow humans on the same day. Often, we sort things out with God and leave the human aspect alone, but that is not scriptural, as we have seen in the two passages. Both are to be done simultaneously.

Questions: Do I have an issue with someone? Have I tried to reconcile with both them and God?

DAY 22

Continuous Offerings

Leviticus 6:8–13 - The LORD spoke to Moses. He said, "***Give Aaron and the priests in his family line a command.*** Tell them, 'Here are some more rules for burnt offerings. The burnt offering must remain on the altar through the whole night. The fire on the altar must be kept burning until morning. The priest must put on his linen clothes. He must put on linen underwear next to his body. He must remove the ashes of the burnt offering that the fire has burned up on the altar. He must place them beside the altar. Then he must take his clothes off and put others on. He must carry the ashes outside the camp to a "clean" place. ***The fire on the altar must be kept burning. It must not go out. Every morning the priest must add more wood to the fire. He must place the burnt offering on the fire.*** He must burn the fat of the friendship offerings on it. ***The fire must be kept burning on the altar all the time. It must not go out.***'"

Jean Kabasomi

The Lord gave Moses instructions for Aaron and the priests concerning the rules for the burnt offerings. One of the instructions given to the priesthood was to ensure that the fire on the altar remained burning continuously. The only way that the fire could burn indefinitely would be if there was a continuous supply of offerings placed on the altar. Here we see that it is the role of the priesthood to ensure that there is always an offering burning on the altar. Today, we too should expect our pastors to be concerned with the continuous supply of offerings in the local church, not because they are looking for wealth, as we are often told by the world, but because, in addition to the role of shepherding, they are also the custodians of our offerings and responsible for the ongoing sacrifices on the altar. We should also note that our sacrifices should not be confined to our monetary giving. This means that we should also expect our pastors to be regularly exhorting us to offer up other sacrifices.

Questions: Am I irritated by my pastor's continuous encouragement to sacrifice? Have I accepted that in addition to praying for me, encouraging me when things get tough – my pastor's role also includes exhorting me to make sacrifices?

DAY 23

Holiness and the Offering

Leviticus 6:24–27 - The Lord spoke to Moses. He said, "Speak to Aaron and the priests in his family line. Tell them, 'Here are some more rules for sin offerings. You must kill the animal for the sin offering in the sight of the Lord. Kill it in the place where the burnt offering is killed. It is very holy. The priest who offers it will eat it. He must eat it in the holy area. He must eat it in the courtyard of the tent of meeting. *Anyone who touches any of its meat will become holy.* Suppose some of the blood is spilled on someone's clothes. Then you must wash them in the holy area.'"

Whenever I attend a more traditional or orthodox church service as a guest, I am always blown away by the respect they have for the things of God. Many of the more traditional churches or High Church services have a reverence for Communion and the utensils used in both the service and in the church building not found in the less traditional wing of the Church. While many of us in the more charismatic or evangelical wings of the Church may find some of the practices legalistic or impractical, there is a need for the things used in the house of God to be viewed and treated as special and holy. In our passage today, we see that just by touching the offerings, the priests were made holy. This shows us that once something is presented to God as a sacrifice, it is no longer just a piece of meat or grain; it is something different in the eyes of God. We, too, should view what we present and offer to God as holy. Whether it is money, our time, home, instruments or service – once it is offered to God, it is holy.

Questions: Do I have a reverence for the things set apart for God's service? Do I see what should be holy as holy because it is used for God?

DAY 24

Full-time Ministry and the Offering

Leviticus 6:18 - ***Any priests in Aaron's family line can eat it.*** It is their share of the food offerings presented to the LORD. It is their share for all time to come. Anyone who touches these offerings will become holy.

In a previous passage, we saw that everybody has a different role in God's house. Rank and order are to be respected not because of anything the person has done, but because that is how God has intended His house to function. In today's passage, we see that the priests in Aaron's line were given a different role. Their position was different from that of all other priests. The priests in Aaron's family were holy – set apart and special because they had a share in the offerings given to God by the people.

How does this translate for us today? This passage reveals to us that there is indeed a difference between priests in full-time ministry and those in lay (part-time) ministry. Both are required and important, but we see here that those who are supported and funded by offerings are automatically set apart and holy because they have 'touched' what belongs to the Lord.

Question: Have I accepted that there is a difference between full-time ministry and lay (voluntary) ministry?

DAY 25

Promotion, Anointing and the Offering

Leviticus 6:19–20 - The LORD spoke to Moses. He said, "On the day each **high priest** in **Aaron's family line is anointed**, he must bring an offering to me. He must bring three and a half pounds of the finest flour as a regular grain offering. He must bring half of it in the morning. He must bring the other half in the evening."

The Lord gave direct instructions on the promotion into the office of high priest. There was only one high priest at any one time. After Aaron, it was to be passed on to one of his sons. On the day of this promotion, the high priest was anointed into this office. The correct response by the newly appointed high priest was to bring an offering to the Lord to mark this promotion.

For Christians, we believe that Christ is the ultimate High Priest, but there is something that can be learnt from this passage. What this reveals to us is that the ideal response to a promotion or new anointing is an offering. Although the promotion for the sons in Aaron's family line was an inheritance and, in a sense, a divine right, they were still expected to present an offering to God. Perhaps God wanted to remind them to be thankful for the position or to remind them that the promotion was in fact because of His decision to give this privilege to Aaron's sons.

Questions: Am I grateful to God for promotions and new positions? Do I remember to give thanks when I begin a new phase in my life? Have I considered giving an offering after a promotion?

DAY 26

Importance of the Sin Offering

Leviticus 7:1–6 - Here are some more rules for guilt offerings. The guilt offering is very holy. You must kill the animal for the guilt offering where you kill the animal for the burnt offering. Splash its blood against the sides of the altar. Offer all its fat. It must include the fat tail and the fat that covers the inside parts. It must include both kidneys with the fat on them next to the lower back muscles. It must also include the long part of the liver. Remove all of it together with the kidneys. The priest must burn all of it on the altar. It is a food offering presented to the LORD. It is a guilt offering. Any male in a priest's family can eat it. But he must eat it in the holy area. It is very holy.

In the first few chapters of Leviticus, it is abundantly clear that sin is a major concern of God. We see that the people of God were required to offer up offerings to account for their sins and to absolve them of their mistakes. The sin offerings also enabled the presence of God to continue to dwell in the camp of the Israelites.

In today's passage, we are told that the guilt offering is very holy to God. When I read this passage, it reminded me of the importance and significance of the sacrifice of Jesus. The guilt and the sin offerings are precisely what Christ came to replace; the *most* special and holy offerings in the eyes of God. It's worth considering here that Christ did not come to replace peace or thanksgiving offerings. He did not come to replace tithes or any other offering, but he came to replace the offering that enables us to commune with and relate to God the Father. Instead of viewing the book of Leviticus as the old legalistic way of doing things, it ought to remind us of the importance and significance of the offering God the Father gave in the form of Jesus Christ in order to have a relationship with each and every one of us.

> John 3:16 - For this is how God loved the world: ***He gave his one and only Son***, so that everyone who believes in him will not perish but have eternal life. (NLT)

Questions: Am I grateful for the gift of salvation through the precious gift of Jesus? Do I understand that his sacrifice was made so that the presence of God can camp with me just as it did with the people of Israel?

DAY 27

Friendship Offerings

Leviticus 7:11 - Here are some more rules for friendship offerings *anyone* may bring to the Lord.

The friendship ('peace' in some translations) offering was open to anyone. This simple verse is a reminder that the Lord is open to friendship and reconciliation with anyone and everyone. We are all welcome and encouraged to begin a relationship with the Lord or to take our relationship with Him to a new and deeper level than where we are now.

Questions: Have I accepted the friendship of God? Do I approach God as a friend? Am I looking for new ways in which to have a deeper and more intimate relationship with the Lord?

DAY 28

Timeliness and Offerings

Leviticus 7:15–18 - Now *as for* the ***flesh of the sacrifice of his thanksgiving peace offerings, it shall be eaten on the day of his offering***; he shall not leave any of it over until morning. But if the sacrifice of his offering is a vow or a voluntary offering, it shall be eaten on the day that he offers his sacrifice, and on the next day what is left of it may be eaten; but what is left over from the flesh of the sacrifice on the third day shall be burned with fire. So if any of the ***flesh of the sacrifice of his peace offerings is ever eaten on the third day, he who offers it will not be accepted, and it will not be credited to him.*** It will be an unclean thing, and the person who eats it shall bear his punishment. (NASB)

Before reading this passage, I had never thought about timeliness and my giving or sacrifices. But, on reflection, it makes perfect sense that the value of any offering decreases if it is not given at the right time.

Let's use an example that we can all understand. We are all grateful for life, but for the majority of us our birthdays are more significant than most of the other days in the year. When we receive gifts on our birthdays, we are grateful, but when we receive gifts for our birthday, it often feels strange. Depending on the length of time after our birthday, we may attribute it to a season or an occasion other than our birthday. A gift received on the day or the day after is very different from a gift received four months later. We find it difficult to attribute it to our birthday. In some instances, the giver may even wait until Christmas or the next birthday to give the gift to the recipient.

I think this is what this passage is getting us to think about. Our thanksgiving to God ought to be timely. When we are prompted to offer up thanksgivings to the Lord, we should do it without hesitation and with the same sort of urgency we have when preparing Christmas or birthday gifts.

Questions: Am I timely with my giving? Does it take me a long time to acknowledge the blessings and gifts that God has placed in my life? Am I grateful to God for what He has done for me?

DAY 29

The Anointing of Others and my Response

Leviticus 7:36 - ***On the day they were anointed, the Lord commanded the Israelites to give*** that part to them. For all time to come, it will be the share of Aaron and the priests in his family line.

On the day of the anointing of the priests in Aaron's line, God commanded the people of Israel to respond by presenting an offering to him. Often, when other people are promoted, we agree and accept that the person promoted should give an offering of thanksgiving. But in this passage, we see that those who are impacted by the promotion are also supposed to give an offering to the Lord. Perhaps this is because the promotion of leadership can lead to promotions, new graces, blessings and open doors for those being led by the newly promoted (anointed). Or perhaps, this passage envisages a more communal approach to blessings and promotion than we display today.

For many of us, promotion is an individual affair. If one person is promoted, it only appears to impact them. Often that person distances themselves from those who have not been promoted. But perhaps God expected the people to respond with an offering because, in a certain sense, they too had been promoted and were supposed to respond accordingly.

Questions: How do *I* respond when other people around me are promoted? Am I grateful to God for a new season in that person's life? Have I asked myself how their promotion might impact me? Am I jealous or envious when others are promoted?

DAY 30

Direction from God

Leviticus 7:37–38 - These are the rules for burnt offerings, grain offerings, sin offerings, guilt offerings and friendship offerings. They are also the rules for the offerings that are given when priests are being prepared to serve the Lord. ***They are the rules the Lord gave Moses on Mount Sinai.*** He gave them on the day he commanded the Israelites to bring their offerings to the Lord. That took place in the Sinai Desert.

The book of Leviticus contains a fair bit of detail; so much so that it is traditionally viewed as legalistic and not applicable. But why does it contain so much detail? Why did God give so many instructions to Moses and Aaron? Perhaps if we take a step back and look from a different perspective, we may see why.

The Lord had just led the people of Israel out of Egypt. They had no government or system for doing things. All that Moses knew was that God required him to lead the people out of Egypt into a new land, but in the book of Leviticus we see the beginnings of God's plan for the people of Israel. The Lord did not just tell Moses to do something: He gave him clear and comprehensive instructions on what was supposed to be done. Rather than an oppressive set of rules, the book of Leviticus should remind us that whenever the Lord gives a vision or dream, He will also give us a blueprint on how we should get that thing done. The book of Leviticus should act as reminder to us that we too are able to get specific direction from God.

Questions: Do I expect God to give me direction for the visions and dreams He has placed in my heart? Have I asked God for direction in my life? Do I look for God's instructions and commands for my life?

Also by Jean Kabasomi

The Greatest Leader of All Time: The Interactions of Jesus according to the Gospel of Matthew

About the Author

Jean Kabasomi is a committed Christian in her local church and works in the City of London. She is the author of *The Greatest Leader of All Time: The Interactions of Jesus according to the Gospel of Matthew*. Jean has two theology degrees – BA Theology from Durham University and MSc Biblical Studies from the University of Edinburgh. You can find out more about Jean at www.jeankabasomi.com. You can connect with Jean on Facebook at www.facebook.com/jeankabasomiauthor.

www.ingramcontent.com/pod-product-compliance
Lightning Source LLC
Chambersburg PA
CBHW071538080526
44588CB00011B/1716